Dr J A Muir Gray and ...

YOUR HEALTH
IN RETIREMENT

AN **A** TO **Z** GUIDE

© 1990 Dr J A Muir Gray & Pat Blair

Published by Age Concern England
Bernard Sunley House
60 Pitcairn Road
Mitcham, Surrey CR4 3LL

Editor   Lee Bennett
Design   Eugenie Dodd
Production   Joyce O'Shaughnessy

Photographs on the cover and on pages
6, 10, 37, 48, 54 Sunil Gupta.

Drawings on pages 17, 26-27 Robin Dodd.

Typeset from disc by Impetus Graphics
Printed by Ebenezer Baylis & Son Ltd,
Worcester

ISBN 0-86242-082-2

Contents

About the Authors

Dr J A Muir Gray is a consultant physician in community medicine for Oxfordshire Health Authority.

Pat Blair has been a medical journalist for many years and has written for specialist magazines and national newspapers. She is the author of *Know Your Medicines* and is vice-chairman of the Medical Journalists' Association.

Introduction

Growing old is a challenge which most people meet successfully. The majority of us are likely to stay fit and active well into our eighties, leading busy lives and playing a full role within the family circle and the local community. Some may encounter new health concerns, such as high blood pressure or heart disease, and have to watch what they eat to a greater extent than before or exercise more regularly. With a little care, such issues need not be a bar to a fulfilling lifestyle.

Whether you are in buoyant good health or having to cope with the effects of disability or illness, the advice given in this book aims to help you look after yourself. The A to Z guide provides details of a wide variety of health-related topics in a frank and honest fashion, giving the information necessary to understand and cope with particular problems.

The section called People to Help You explains the services provided by the National Health Service, the local authority and complementary medical practitioners, whilst Useful Organisations gives a brief description of, and the addresses for, a large number of advice agencies – all keen to work with you in maintaining your health in retirement.

AN A TO Z

This section of the book contains information on how to maintain and improve your well-being even if you suffer from a chronic illness, such as heart disease, requiring specialised medical treatment. You can keep the unaffected parts of the body as healthy as possible by watching your weight, using medicine sensibly and following the advice given about exercise and preventive health care.

These suggestions will help you to live as comfortably as possible with conditions that may restrict your movements and interfere with daily living tasks such as bathing and dressing. The effect of ageing is also considered in relation to topics such as sexuality, mental health and exercise. In addition, there is guidance about when to seek professional help.

Alzheimer's disease
SEE Confusion

Anxiety

Everyone knows what it is to be anxious – you feel apprehensive and can't concentrate because of disquieting thoughts. Some people develop tension headaches, others get stomach pains; some get the urge to pass water, or even suffer diarrhoea. Some unfortunate people experience all these symptoms.

The main cause of anxiety is uncertainty, perhaps about health or money or what will happen in the future. Although anxiety is a normal reaction to certain situations, some people get anxious more easily and are difficult to reassure. In general, the characteristic does not change with age – if you were a young worrier, you are likely to be an old worrier.

What you can do   Worries seem more daunting when you are alone and have no one with whom to discuss them. Anxiety can be lessened by finding someone to talk to like a trusted neighbour, friend, or relative, your doctor or a health visitor.

Getting professional help   If feelings of anxiety interfere with your appetite or sleep for more than two days, you should see the doctor. If you start believing that other people are trying to poison or kill you – you should seek medical advice at once.

The doctor may help merely by listening and suggesting ways for coping with anxiety, such as relaxation exercises. These involve concentrating on breathing while you tense and relax all the muscles in your body. Medicine to lessen anxiety should only be prescribed after other possible solutions have been tried. Unfortunately tranquillising drugs are used too frequently in the treatment of anxiety.

Arthritis

There are three main types of arthritis: rheumatoid, which usually comes on in middle age; osteoarthritis, which is common in old age; and gout, which is not caused by drinking too much or living too well but which can result in a build-up of uric acid in the joints.

What you can do   Although joints are damaged by arthritis, it is possible to prevent them being injured further if you keep your weight down, and thereby reduce the pressure on joints, and keep yourself mobile.

You should also exercise as much as possible without straining a painful joint. Swimming is particularly good, as is cycling provided the arthritis is not severe. However, jogging or any other exercise which bangs the joints is not advisable.

If you have pain in one joint, rest it for a few hours; and for an aching ankle or knee, keep your leg propped up comfortably above hip height. Keep the affected area warm by holding a covered hot water bottle next to it. If you need painkillers more than once a week, get in touch with the doctor.

Getting professional help   If the joint stiffness, pain and weakness of arthritis are marked, your doctor may arrange physiotherapy or, in severe cases, the replacement of a damaged joint with an artificial one. Hip replacement is now a common and safe operation, although the waiting lists for it are very long in many parts of the country.

Bathing

A rubber mat in the bath to prevent slipping is particularly important for people who have difficulty getting in and out of the bath as hips become stiff or if they are unsteady on their feet.

What you can do   Someone with very stiff hips should have a grab rail fitted across the bath or attached to the wall next to it, or have a pole fitted to the floor and ceiling beside the bath. Another useful aid is a padded seat at the end of the bath or fitted securely inside.

Ask the occupational therapist (OT) for advice about bathing aids and adapting your bathroom for a disability. There *may* be financial help available for aids and adaptations, and the social services department or the OT will have information about what equipment is free.

If you need a bath aid in a hurry, you can borrow one from the Red Cross or through the local Disablement Information and Advice line. Also contact the Disabled Living Foundation (address on page 65) for complete information about aids for daily living.

Getting professional help   The district nurse can help people who are unable to wash themselves all over, but most nurses are too busy to provide more than a weekly bath.

Bronchitis and emphysema

Bronchitis is an inflammation of the tubes which carry air to the lungs, while emphysema damages the delicate sponge-like tissues of the lungs. Both diseases interfere with the amount of oxygen which gets into the blood, and that in turn cuts down on the body's ability to do its work. The symptoms of both disorders are coughing and bringing up phlegm and breathlessness. With emphysema there is often a wheezing cough and breathing can become very restricted.

What you can do   If you are a smoker, you should stop, as it is never too late to benefit from giving up the habit. Also try to keep your weight down by watching your diet and taking as much exercise as you can. Ask the hospital doctor or physiotherapist which type of exercise is best for people with lung disease.

Getting professional help   The doctor may prescribe medicines (including inhalers and antibiotics) to take on a long-term basis or when your condition gets worse, usually as a result of catching a cold or suffering from another chest ailment.

Make sure you get an influenza jab every winter. If you get 'flu or catch a cold, see your doctor as soon as possible.

SEE ALSO Smoking

Cancer

Many people talk about cancer as if it was all one disease. There are, however, many different types, each of which has its own symptoms, treatment and outlook. The most common are: cancer of the lungs and throat; cancers of the bowel; cancers that affect women – cervical or cancer of the breast; and skin cancer.

If you have had cancer diagnosed, the outlook is not as gloomy as many people believe. It should not be regarded as a death sentence, because if diagnosed and treated early enough, some cancers can be halted. In fact, many older people who develop cancer will not be killed by it but will die from something else. Cancer treatment is becoming more effective, and recent developments have resulted in much better control of pain and other symptoms through drugs.

What you can do   The symptoms of the different cancers vary widely, but there are certain ones you should report immediately to the doctor: passing blood, either in vomit, in sputum, in bowel waste (faeces), in urine, or from the vagina; an unexplained loss of weight; hoarseness that persists for more than two weeks; a sudden lump in the breast or a change in its shape or size or the colour of the nipple. If you have a sore on your lips, tongue or face that does not heal or is getting bigger, go to see your doctor.

Getting professional help   To detect the presence of cervical cancer, a smear test is available to women under the age of 65 every three years. If you are over 65 and have never had a cervical smear, you should ask the doctor whether one is necessary. The test can be done by a GP or a well woman or family planning clinic.

Cancer of the breast can be treated successfully if detected early enough. Free mammography (breast X-ray) is available every three years to women aged between 50 and 64, who should receive a computerised reminder about this. If you are 65 and have any cause for concern, you should ask the doctor for a test to be arranged.

There is no routine screening test for cancer affecting male organs. If you notice any changes, for example, lumps or tenderness in your testicles, seek your doctor's advice. If you have difficulty in passing urine or experience any pain, you should also ask the doctor, as these can be signs of prostatic cancer.

Skin cancers, which are becoming more common as a result of people taking intensive 'sun-soaked' holidays, can also be treated successfully if detected early enough. If you have a pigmented patch on your skin and can answer 'yes' to three or more of the following points, you should consult your doctor: does the pigmented patch itch or feel abnormal? Is it 1cm or more in diameter and increasing in size? Does the density of black and brown colour vary? Is it inflamed, bleeding or crusting?

Caring for someone

Stress or strain can affect the health of those who have constantly to care for someone else, especially if they struggle along too long on their own. Early signs of stress include: irritability, either with the person you look after or with others; headaches or other physical symptoms; constant tiredness, particularly if your sleep is disturbed; loss of appetite; feeling depressed and frequently being tearful. You might be less loving towards the person you are helping, even if only momentarily, or feel tense or desperate.

What you can do   If you feel any such strains, you should seek help, not only for your own good but also for your dependant's sake. Discuss the problems with the health visitor or anyone else you trust. Often, sharing problems will give you relief.

You may need to explain to the person you are looking after, that you also need help because of the strain of constant caring.

Getting professional help   If you have too many things to do in caring for someone, the GP or social worker may be able to organise other services. These could include a home help, a care attendant or sitting service to enable you to get out or have some time to yourself. Perhaps there is an adaptation for your home or a laundry service that would make caring easier.

The social services department may be able to arrange for the person you are looking after to have day care or occasionally to stay overnight or for a week or two in a special home or hostel. For someone who needs constant care, a short stay in a hospital – sometimes on a regular basis – may be arranged to give you a break.

Getting the support of others   To get the help you need, find an ally – for example, the community health council can help with health service problems; and the local Age Concern group or Citizen's Advice Bureau will have information about local services. Also get in touch with the Carer's National Association at the address on page 63.

Try to keep calm, no matter how annoying officials or professionals appear to be. Get the name of every official you contact. Write rather than telephone, except in emergencies, and keep a copy of your letters. If you are going to social services or the housing department, unless it is in an emergency, make an appointment first, to save time and effort.

You may want to make a formal complaint through the community health council or the family practitioner committee (see page 52).

Colds and 'flu

Infections like colds and 'flu are not difficult to recognise, and you can usually treat most of the symptoms yourself.

What you can do   Treat a cough with a steam inhalation, or for a dry cough, use linctus. Contact the doctor if the cough continues for more than two weeks, if there is blood in the sputum or if it is greenish in colour, if you get breathless or have chest pains.

Because infections weaken the body, don't force yourself to do tiring work or expose yourself to bad weather while you are feeling unwell.

Rest and keep warm, and after 48 hours you should feel better. If not, call a doctor.

Drink plenty of fluids: Bovril, Ribena, tonic water, tea, soup – whatever you enjoy – but be careful of milk or cream if you feel sick. Do not force yourself to eat, and try not to worry about constipation – you should not expect to have a bowel movement if you are not eating.

Give your body time to recover during the first few weeks following the illness, but do not spend all your time sitting back either. Take short walks, and stretch your shoulders, elbows and hands which tend to stiffen if you have been sitting or lying down. If your joints become stiff, see the doctor.

If you also suffer from diabetes, bronchitis, emphysema or heart disease, consult your doctor immediately when you catch a cold or 'flu.

Confusion

Someone who is unable to remember the names of acquaintances, items on a shopping list or what he or she has gone into another room to collect is not necessarily suffering from the symptoms of early dementia. However, if they are unable to remember the name of close relatives or an address, this is not normal and a doctor should be consulted. Do note, though, that a common feature of confusion is for the person affected to lose the ability to notice these changes in behaviour and to reject the need for treatment.

There are two types of confusion: the type that comes on quickly – within a few days or weeks someone gets noticeably forgetful or confused – is likely to be connected with some treatable ailment, such as a chest infection, heart failure or poorly controlled diabetes. It could also be a side-effect of some medicine being taken, and the problem should be discussed with a doctor, health visitor or district nurse.

Confusion that develops slowly over a few years, is likely to result from dementia, which causes permanent damage to brain cells and is not treatable at the present time. The most common dementia is Alzheimer's disease, the second most common being multi-infarct dementia due to an impaired blood supply to the brain. This type of confusion can also be caused by vitamin deficiency, thyroid disease, alcohol abuse, by not eating properly or by being cold.

A person who seems to have dementia but who cries a lot, feels sad and needs comfort may also require a doctor's opinion to determine whether he or she is severely depressed rather than suffering from dementia.

What you can do   People who are looking after a relative or friend with dementia need a great deal of support and guidance in using services and getting a break. There may be a local carers' support group or Alzheimer's Disease Society group (see page 61 for national headquarters). For information about day and night sitting services respite and day care, meals on wheels, get in touch with the Carer's National Association (address on page 63) or a local Age Concern group.

Dementia is a sad fact of life for sufferers and for those looking after them. Encourage the person to take an interest in day-to-day affairs and encourage the use of memory aids like shopping lists and simple ways to remember the date and time of day.

By using such techniques, you are helping to remind the dementia sufferer of the real world around them. To reinforce communication, keep the person's possessions such as ornaments or photos in sight, and make sure that it is clear where the lavatory is. A free booklet entitled *Who Cares?*, available from the Health Education Authority and local health education units, offers excellent advice and suggestions (address on page 66).

Getting professional help   There is no specific treatment available for dementia. For someone with confusion that has come on quickly, ask the doctor to check on other illnesses which lead to similar symptoms and can be treated. The person's hearing and eyesight should also be checked, as impairment can contribute to confusion.

The doctor may also refer the dementia sufferer to the psychiatric service for assessment. They may need to go to a day hospital for part of the week or be put on the waiting list for long-term hospital care.

SEE ALSO Caring for someone

The fibre contained in fresh fruit, vegetables, wholemeal bread and cereals is essential for keeping your bowels moving normally.

Constipation

You are constipated when you have to strain to pass stools. For some people, a bowel movement every two or three days is normal and healthy, while for others a daily movement is normal. It is important to be aware of any changes in usual habits, whether you go once a day or every other day.

What you can do   A regular intake of fibre, will help to keep bowels moving normally. Fibre is contained in fruit and vegetables or in the bran in wholemeal bread and flour and breakfast cereals. It can also help to add unprocessed bran to cereal mixtures, porridge, soups or stews. The amount needed to produce a comfortably passed motion varies – try a dessert-spoonful a day to start with and adjust as needed. It is unwise to take large amounts of bran all at once.

Keeping active and drinking enough fluids will also encourage a normal bowel movement.

Getting professional help If there is a decrease in your normal frequency which lasts for a week, discuss the problem with your pharmacist, who should be able to recommend a laxative. This can be helpful occasionally, but in the long term, increasing the amount of fibre and fluids in your diet is the best remedy. If your bowel action does not return rapidly to normal, see your doctor.

If constipation is sudden and you also have stomach pains or are vomiting, see the doctor immediately. Similarly, you should consult the doctor if there is a sudden increase in the number of times you go or if there is pain , or you are passing blood or mucus.

SEE ALSO Incontinence

Deafness

SEE Hearing

Dental care

Even though many people aged over 60 in Britain do not have their natural teeth, it is important to have dental checks so that any change in your mouth can be seen and, if necessary, dentures adjusted or replaced. The commonest cause of losing teeth is gum disease.

What you can do Correct tooth brushing technique with a soft toothbrush should always clean the surface of the gums as well as the teeth. Ask the dentist or dental hygienist if you are unsure how good your own technique is. To help remove large particles of food that get lodged in the spaces between teeth, use dental floss. You can also do this with interdental sticks which are especially useful for massaging the gums.

If you have very large spaces between your teeth, try using a toothbrush with a single point to clean between the teeth as well as the gum surface.

Getting professional help   If you have some or all of your natural teeth, you should have a dental check at least once a year. If you wear dentures, have them checked every three years. After natural teeth are lost, gums shrink rapidly at first and more slowly later. The shape of the mouth changes to some extent, and dentures should be adjusted at regular intervals to prevent sore gums and damage from ill-fitting dentures.

Any soreness or lumps on the gums should always be looked at by a dentist. Most are easily cured, but if neglected they can become serious.

Cost of treatment   Before starting treatment you should ensure that the dentist understands that you want National Health Service treatment and agrees to provide it. The only way to be certain about this is to sign the contract form, which requires your NHS number, before treatment starts. If that is not done, the dentist can ask for private fees.

Even under the NHS you may have to pay for the initial examination and treatment, and a charge is normally made for replacement dentures. However, if you are on a very low income or receive income support or are in hospital, you are entitled to a free examination and treatment.

Depression

Everyone gets depressed from time to time, but older people seem to suffer more from depression. This may be a response to bereavement or a disabling disease. However, this does not mean that depression in old age is inevitable or untreatable. If you become depressed or see the symptoms in someone else, do not accept that it is just part of getting older or that it will go away naturally.

The physical symptoms that accompany depression are pain, loss of appetite and weight and insomnia. In addition, there may be frequent complaints about loneliness and prolonged grief expressed by someone who has recently experienced the death of a partner. Someone who drinks more than usual, talks only about feeling low, and becomes agitated and confused is severely depressed and should get professional help. In contrast, some depressed people become very 'slowed down' and apathetic.

What you can do   Avoid being isolated – the more involved you are with others, the less likely you are to be depressed. Try to keep your mind active by taking a course in some subject you've always wanted to know about. Find ways of helping other people, perhaps by doing some local voluntary work.

Getting professional help   If a depressed friend or relative says that they are thinking of 'ending it all', they should be taken seriously, and you should consult their doctor immediately. Suicide is more common in old age than in younger age groups.

If you feel depressed for longer than usual, try to identify the cause and discuss your feelings with a person you trust – the GP, a home help, a friend or someone connected with your religion. If you are depressed because of the physical dependency connected with arthritis, for example, you may want to discuss this with the occupational therapist.

Sometimes anti-depressant drugs are necessary to lift depression, but the doctor should only prescribe these when the opportunity to talk to a trusted person has also been tried.

SEE ALSO Mental health

Diabetes

This is a common condition in old age which occurs when the pancreas does not produce enough insulin to regulate the amount of blood sugar the body contains. The type of diabetes that develops in older people does not usually require insulin but may be controlled by losing weight. Although it may not cause any symptoms, people with the disease may develop skin and urinary infections more frequently and may suffer from impaired eyesight.

What you can do   As people who are overweight run a greater risk of developing diabetes, weight control is important. There is no special diabetic diet; and the guidelines for Weight control (page 47) apply just as much to those with diabetes. In brief: eat regular meals, enough to help you keep or maintain your ideal weight; increase your intake of high-carbohydrate, high-fibre foods; cut down on sugary foods and fat; moderate the amount of salt you take; drink alcohol in moderation.

Because diabetes can lead to other complications, it is particularly important for the sufferer to be careful about skin abrasions or minor cuts, expecially on hands or feet, which could develop into a severe infection.

Getting professional help   Someone who suffers repeated urinary infections or has skin eruptions that do not heal quickly, should ask the doctor to check for diabetes. If you have diabetes, pay particular attention to foot care; it may be advisable to get professional help with, for example, trimming toenails, to prevent the risk of a cut and then infection developing.

Checks on the level of sugar in the blood can be done at home through regular testing of urine or a droplet of blood. Your doctor can show you how to do this. Make sure you also get regular check-ups from your doctor or, if possible, a diabetic clinic. For some people, weight control is not enough, and their doctor may prescribe sugar-lowering tablets.

SEE ALSO Foot care

Diarrhoea and vomiting

Both these symptoms can have many causes – eg, excessive eating or drinking, infections and food poisoning.

Diarrhoea can result from eating too much bran, taking too many laxatives or as an unwanted effect of taking antibiotics.

What you can do   If you are unable to keep down any medicine which you need to take regularly, get advice from the pharmacist, the doctor or district nurse.

Drink plenty of fluid in small amounts at a time (plain water is best for diarrhoea). Don't force yourself to eat any food that is supposed to stop vomiting or diarrhoea. Don't prepare food for other people while you are suffering from either of these symptoms.

Getting professional help   Frail elderly people should contact the doctor immediately if diarrhoea and vomiting persist for more than two hours. Others should ask for help if they are not better after 24 hours.

Get in touch immediately with the doctor if you pass blood or mucus and if you have pain.

Food hygiene   Much of the food poisoning that occurs could be prevented by being aware of the following guidelines when preparing food. Hands should always be washed beforehand, and preparation surfaces should be kept clean. To reduce food-borne illness, the bacteria causing it, such as salmonella, must be prevented from growing. Most bacteria grow best at temperatures between 10° and 60°C, so food should be kept at temperatures above or below that 'danger zone'. Cooked meat or poultry should be eaten immediately, kept above 60°C, or cooled within an hour and then stored in the fridge.

Keep raw and cooked foods separately in the fridge or cupboard, preferably on separate shelves. This prevents bacteria in the raw food from being transferred to the cooked food. To prevent indirect contamination, do not prepare raw and cooked foods on the same chopping board or surface: clean the board after preparing each type of food. Frozen meat and poultry should be thawed thoroughly before cooking. If reheating prepared foods, including soups, they should be piping hot all the way through.

Disability

If you suffer from some chronic disease or condition such as heart disease or arthritis, it does not mean you can never take exercise or become fitter. You can benefit from exercise and thereby avoid immobility, muscle weakness, stiff joints and breathlessness. Ask your doctor which exercise is best for your particular problem.

What you can do   Make sure that you are getting all the medical treatment you need, also that you are getting all the financial help available such as attendance or mobility allowance. The Age Concern book *Your Rights* gives full details about all State benefits for retired people. It can be purchased from local Age Concern groups or from Age Concern England at the address on page 78.

If you can stand and are able to walk, try to increase your walking ability, and maintain strength and suppleness in your upper arms and body by doing special exercises. Do as much housework as you can – that means a little bit more than you can do easily. Also try the suggestions for gentle exercise for people with movement problems outlined in *The Magic of Movement* (details on page 74).

If you are confined to a chair and unable to stand up, practise movements to strengthen and loosen your spinal column, neck, shoulders, arms and hands. You may also be able to attend a day centre or day hospital which offers exercise classes. The health visitor can advise on this.

Try doing things for yourself, rather than have things done for you, even if you do have to struggle a little to succeed. Explain to other people who want to do everything for you that you would like to do as much as possible yourself.

Getting professional help　Your GP is the main channel of advice and help for an illness that causes disability. You can also approach other professionals such as the district nurse and the occupational therapist. The Disabled Living Foundation (address on page 65) is the key agency to contact for information about a wide range of aids for daily living.

Dressing

People with a disability who are otherwise capable of looking after themselves sometimes need help with dressing and undressing. They may have difficulty in coping with hooks and eyes or buttons, because of arthritic hands. Joint stiffness also interferes with putting on socks, tying shoelaces, fastening underwear or pulling things over the head.

What you can do　Your choice of clothes is important. Women may find it easier to manage a front-fastening bra, and men may cope with braces better than a trouser belt. Clothing can be adapted to make dressing easier – for example, if buttons or zips are a problem on skirts and trousers, they could be replaced by Velcro fastenings. It is possible to buy clothes specially designed for people with disabilities. For more information contact the Disabled Living Foundation at the address on page 65.

Getting professional help   A nurse, physiotherapist and occupational therapist can give advice on dressing for particular problems and on adapting clothes. If you are completely unable to dress, even with that help, the community nursing service *may* be able to offer daily assistance.

SEE ALSO Bathing

Drink problems

A little alcohol does you no harm unless you are overweight, do not eat properly, or have a health condition that is made worse by alcohol. It is worth noting as well that tolerance to drink decreases with age and that alcohol does react with some medicines, especially sleeping tablets, antibiotics and tranquillisers. Check with your doctor or pharmacist about whether alcohol can affect any medication you take – whether bought over the counter or prescribed.

■ **As a guideline, the recommended weekly limits for safe drinking are:**

For older men: 4 to 6 units, 2 to 3 times a week or about 2 units a day.

For older women: 2 to 3 units, 2 to 3 times a week or 1 or 2 units a day.

A unit is: a half pint of beer or lager; a glass of wine; a single measure of spirits (standard pub measure).

Experts disagree about the yardstick to use in deciding whether someone has a drink problem. Changes in a person's state of health such as shakiness, confusion or loss of memory can be wrongly assumed to be part of 'getting old' when they may be signs of heavy drinking.

What you can do   If you are drinking more than you used to because of the effect it has and this is causing physical, mental or financial problems – even if you only admit them to yourself – ask for help from your doctor, from friends or from a local Alcoholics Anonymous counselling group.

Ears
SEE Hearing

Emphysema
SEE Bronchitis

Exercise

One of the aims of exercise is to increase fitness so that you respond to physical challenges without stress. A fit person is able to climb stairs without panting, or rake leaves for, say, half an hour, without straining muscles and feeling stiff.

Another important aspect of exercise is improved co-ordination which shows in your ability to move more confidently and to be less likely to fall. Exercise also helps you to sleep better, promotes a healthy appetite and keeps down weight.

By following a regular exercise programme you will increase: stamina (involving your heart and lungs and the ability to carry on any activity without having to stop for breath); strength (involving muscles and being able to keep going without having to rest frequently); suppleness (involving muscles and joints and being able to exercise without being stiff the next day).

How often to exercise   The best rule is 'little and often' as the older you are, the more easily you become unfit. Even a few days without exercise will make you feel stiff and weaker. Housework and gardening use leg and arm muscles, but you should also do some vigorous activity every day to make your pulse and rate of breathing faster.

Start with only a minute or two's exertion and increase the amount slowly. Try walking briskly from one lamp post to another, then walk at your normal pace for the next three before another brisk walk. Ask the doctor about any discomfort, pain or breathlessness.

Exercising your arms and shoulders

1 Sit on a chair and lift your arms up sideways so that the sides of the arms touch your ears. Keep the arm muscles flexed and strong. Lower your arms sideways.

2 Then raise your arms up in front of you to shoulder height. Hold weights or try cans in your hands to help increase your strength. Lower arms slowly to your sides.

3 Without weights in your hands, raise your arms sideways and clap them above your head. Look up at your hands when doing this. Lower your arms.

4 Take up the weights again, and slowly raise your arms sideways, as in the first exercise, twisting arms inwards and outwards as you do so. Continue to twist the arms as you lower them to your sides.

5 Finally, stand up with your arms at your sides and without weights in your hands. Raise your shoulders up as high as you can. Then lower them.

6 Then push your shoulders forwards and backwards so that the shoulder blades come together at the back.

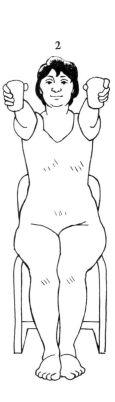

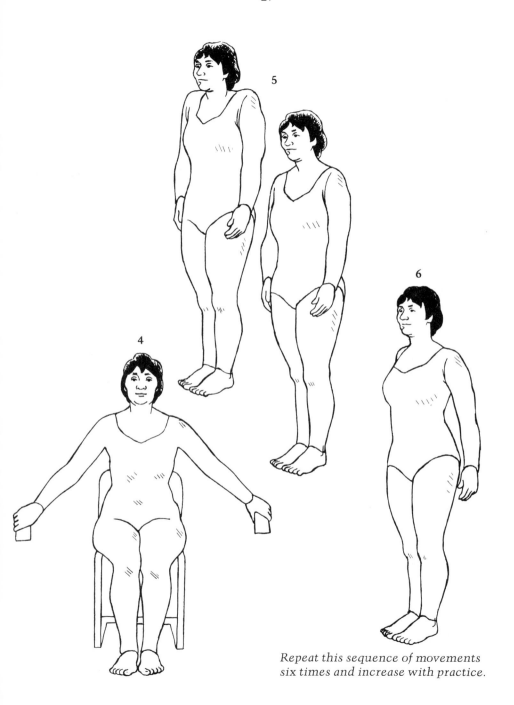

Repeat this sequence of movements six times and increase with practice.

If you have joint problems, be careful of exercises which 'bang' the joints. If you are confined to the house, or cannot get around unaided, you may be able to attend a day centre for exercise classes. Ask the health visitor who may also be able to put you in touch with a means of transport, if that is a problem.

If you have heart disease, high blood pressure, bronchitis or emphysema – or any other chronic disease – but want to improve your fitness, check with your doctor before you start any exercise which makes you breathless and increases pulse rate.

If you are concerned about when to give up exercise in old age, keep this guideline in mind: if you've always been physically active, you should continue to cycle, swim, climb mountains, cut the grass as long as you are able – even if you find the activity more difficult. As long as a sport or activity remains enjoyable, carry on with it, provided you experience only gradual difficulty.

Types of exercise   Cycling, like swimming, is good for people with arthritis who find that a brisk walk produces painful joints. Cycling improves strength and stamina but does not increase suppleness to any great degree. However, if you are taking it up again after a number of years, do note that you will not be able to accelerate or get out of the path of other vehicles as quickly as when you were younger.

Dancing maintains and improves strength, stamina, co-ordination and suppleness, especially modern and jazz dancing. Try devising your own dance routines at home as a regular feature of listening to a tape or music on the radio.

Jogging in later life is best left to those who have been doing it for a number of years. Rather than starting to jog at age 50 or over, take brisk walks instead which are less jarring to hips and knees.

Swimming improves most aspects of fitness. If you already know how to swim but feel self-conscious about your appearance or strokes, try joining an over-50s club or a class to improve your skill and enjoyment.

Walking strengthens leg muscles and increases stamina provided you walk briskly. However, it is of only limited value for increasing suppleness unless you take really long strides and swing your arms for ten or twenty paces or take ten deep breaths – expanding your lungs to their full capacity – every ten yards. If walking is your main form of exercise, try to combine it with keep-fit or dancing to improve suppleness as well.

Yoga is one of the best forms of exercise for older people, and includes a period of mental relaxation which is useful in relieving stress. Tai Chi and aerobics are also designed to improve stamina, strength, suppleness and skill; and many keep-fit classes now teach gentle flowing exercises, often set to music, that are ideal for older people.

SEE ALSO Disability

Eyesight

As you grow older, the lens of the eye loses its elasticity. The result is that small print becomes blurred when held at the normal reading distance, but can be brought into focus by holding the book at arm's length. This is a normal change.

Some people assume that any change in their vision is due to ageing, but that is not the case; and complete loss of vision is uncommon. However, many older people develop one of the three common eye diseases of old age: cataract (a clouding of the lens); glaucoma (when fluid inside the eyeball increases) and macular degeneration (which affects the retina). Diabetes can also impair your sight.

What you can do You should ensure that your home is adequately lighted for reading and sewing and that there is proper lighting over stairs or in an area where you are likely to trip. You should also get rid of small rugs and repair any loose edges on carpets or lino floors.

Have your eyes tested every two years provided you do not notice anything going wrong. However, do not wait until your two years are up if you are finding it more difficult to read, thread a needle, read bus numbers, or if you notice any other change in your vision.

Getting professional help The following symptoms are not normal and should be checked with your doctor or optician: double vision; black spots or areas of darkness; pain in the eye; seeing colours, or haloes round the edges of objects; redness of the eye; sudden loss of the ability to see clearly.

Cataract and glaucoma are both treatable, the first with an operation and the second with eye drops, tablets, or surgery. Laser treatment is often used to halt the eye changes that occur in diabetes.

Cost of treatment   Opticians may now make a charge for a sight test. However, you will be able to have a free test if you receive income support or if you belong to a priority group, which includes the registered blind and partially sighted, diabetics and people who have glaucoma and their close relatives aged 40 or more.

Provided you are receiving income support or are on a low income, you are entitled to a voucher towards the cost of glasses. The voucher carries a financial value linked to your optical prescription and can be used as part-payment for a pair of glasses.

Foot care

The fitter you are, the less likely you are to suffer from painful feet – strong leg muscles help support the arch of the foot and prevent aching.

What you can do   The first step to good foot health is to make sure your shoes are broad and long enough and that tights, stockings or socks do not compress the toes.

Keep the skin in good order by washing your feet daily, without steeping them in water. Pat them dry, making sure they are thoroughly dry between the toes. Immediately after washing is a good time to trim toenails. Cut them straight across and use a file if the nail becomes really thick and horny.

Athlete's foot, a fungal infection, can be treated by applying surgical spirit between the toes after washing. If the problem does not clear, use an antifungal cream or lotion, which is obtainable from the pharmacist.

For complete guidance about foot conditions, and adapting shoes for comfort, see *The Foot Care Book* (details on page 74).

Getting professional help   There are certain foot conditions which you should not attempt to treat yourself. If any part of the foot becomes inflamed, swollen or painful or if the colour of the skin becomes white, dusky red or purple, contact your doctor as soon as possible, because the blood circulation to the foot may be affected.

Minor foot ailments, if left untreated, can become more serious when you have circulation problems or a condition such as diabetes, which leaves you more prone to infections. In such cases, it is not advisable to use corn plasters on corns or to treat corns with a razor blade or other implements. Consult a chiropodist about corns, cuts or abrasions that do not heal within a few days. If you cannot get an appointment with a state registered chiropodist, ask the doctor or district nurse to help.

People with diabetes must have regular chiropody – about every six months – as they may be unable to see or feel skin damages on their feet.

Cost of treatment   NHS chiropody services are free to everyone over the age of 60, but health authorities vary in the extent of provision. Some are unable, because of a shortage of state registered chiropodists, to provide a comprehensive service. There may be a delay in being seen and you may want to consider private treatment. For information about qualified chiropodists, see page 53.

Hearing

Some loss of ability to hear high-pitched sounds, such as the telephone, is common in old age. If you are unable to follow a conversation with several people talking, that is not normal. Deafness is a serious affliction because it is a barrier to normal conversation, but much can be done to cope with hearing difficulties. Often the main obstacle is embarrassment and the reluctance to admit you cannot hear. A common cause of deafness is wax, which the doctor can relieve by syringing. Do not poke anything into your ear to try to clear the wax yourself.

What you can do   If you are hard of hearing, you should explain to people how they can help – by speaking slowly and clearly and as normally as possible, not louder. Get them to sit facing the light so you can see their lips more easily and to sit on your better side if you can hear better with one ear. Reduce background noise where possible by turning down the radio or TV or closing doors to keep sounds out.

You may also benefit from such aids as a telephone with a flashing light as well as a ring, or a light which flashes when the doorbell goes.

Getting professional help   If hearing difficulties have nothing to do with wax or an infection, the GP may refer you to a hearing aid centre or to an ear nose and throat (ENT) clinic at the hospital to check whether you need a hearing aid. Do be aware that there are long waiting lists for services provided by the NHS for hearing aids. An aid is an amplifier and will not restore perfect hearing.

If you have tinnitus (ringing in the ears) a tinnitus masker may help. You may want to contact the tinnitus support service which is run by the Royal National Institute for the Deaf (address on page 70). Some people with impaired hearing also benefit from a lip-reading class to learn the basic skills. A social worker for the deaf can advise about this, or contact the Association of Teachers of Lipreading at the address on page 62.

Cost of aids   NHS hearing aids are available on free loan, and replacements and batteries are also free. Private hearing aids are expensive. Do not buy one through an advertisement unless you have first checked with the ENT clinic or the GP about what is suitable and a recommended supplier. You could also contact the Royal National Institute for the Deaf.

Heart disease

Coronary heart disease, the most common disorder affecting the heart, is caused by the narrowing of the arteries that supply the heart with blood. It can lead to angina, a chest pain that comes on during any exertion. The two other common heart diseases are a weakness of the heart muscle and a disorder of its rhythm, which can cause blackouts. A heart attack is the common name for a blockage, perhaps a blood clot, which shuts off the flow of blood to a section of the heart muscle. Any of these disorders can lead to heart failure.

What you can do　Almost everyone who is going to be troubled by heart disease will already have it by the time they are 65. Prevention must therefore start at a much earlier age. However, it is usually possible to prevent a heart condition getting worse: weight control, stopping smoking and taking exercise all help.

What sort of exercise you can take, and how much, depends on the particular heart condition you have, so be guided by your doctor. In general, walking (up to three miles a day) and swimming are ideal.

Excess weight puts extra strain on the heart by making it work harder to pump the blood around, which is why weight control is important. Keep your weight steady or, if possible, lose some. Eat less fat overall (particularly the saturated fats found in dairy foods, in red meat, in some margarine and hard cooking fats) and switch to unsaturated fats. Influenza also puts a strain on the heart, so ask your doctor in the autumn whether a 'flu injection is right for you.

Getting professional help　Many people with heart disease have their symptoms controlled by medicines, including in some cases a daily dose of aspirin. Some people with heart disease are at a greater risk of suffering a heart attack. If you get a severe chest pain, accompanied by breathlessness, sweating and a feeling of faintness, you should get medical help immediately.

As a long-term treatment for heart disease, coronary by-pass operations are common and safe. In that operation, a piece of vein from the leg is used to by-pass the narrowed piece of artery in the heart.

Cardiac pacemakers help people with irregular slow heartbeats. They are painless and can transform the affected person's life.

SEE ALSO Weight control

Incontinence

Incontinence is not a normal part of ageing. Few people pass water or open their bowels without warning, though this can occur after a stroke, or it may be a side-effect of some medicines. More commonly, incontinence occurs when there is a decrease in the warning time between when you 'want' to go and when you 'have' to go, and mobility can affect the time it takes you to reach the toilet. Each factor on its own can also cause incontinence.

In men, urgency is usually due to prostate trouble which also has other signs such as difficulty in starting the stream which is not as forceful as it once was; or dribbling at the end of the stream, instead of stopping quickly and cleanly. All these are abnormal signs, not 'old age', and should be discussed with the GP, with a view toward receiving surgical treatment. Eventually a man with an enlarged prostate may become unable to pass urine at all.

In women, common causes of urgency are urinary infection and stress incontinence – weakness of the muscles of the pelvis, as a result of stretching during labour in childbirth. Pelvic muscles are sometimes so weak that a little urine leaks out of the bladder whenever you cough, laugh or sneeze.

What you can do   Where incontinence is a matter of not reaching the toilet in time, you could try timing your trips – say, every hour or so – and if necessary using a walking aid to help you get there more quickly. If removing clothing is difficult, see the entry on 'Dressing' for adapting clothing.

If the room where you spend most of your time during the days is too far from the lavatory, you may be able to turn your bedroom into a living-room or vice versa. For night time, a urinal bottle or a commode next to the bed can be useful.

Getting professional help   Incontinence is usually curable, so try to overcome your embarrassment about the problem and ask for advice. Prostate trouble can be cured by simple and safe treatment. Stress incontinence is helped by doing special exercises. The continence adviser at the Disabled Living foundation can send instructions for these. Many women do not seek help early enough because they believe, wrongly, that stress incontinence is due to old age.

Some health authorities employ continence advisers, nurses trained to advise about all problems connected with incontinence. The doctor or health visitor should know whether there is a continence adviser in your area. A continence adviser will explain about the best sort of personal protection (pads, pants and other aids).

Indigestion

People who say they have indigestion may have several different complaints. A common one is a pain in the upper abdomen, sometimes with wind. Another is a burning sensation behind the breastbone, made worse by lying down, bending or sitting in a slouched position; this is sometimes called 'heartburn' and happens because normal stomach acids run back into the gullet. Indigestion symptoms may follow unwise eating and can be made worse by anxiety.

What you can do   Get an antacid mixture (eg, magnesium trisilicate) from the chemist and take it according to the instructions on the bottle. Liquid mixtures tend to be more effective than indigestion tablets. For heartburn, take a dose of the mixture before going to bed, and try raising the bed head so that you sleep with your head higher than your stomach: the acid cannot then run uphill into your gullet.

Getting professional help   If your symptoms persist for longer than a few days, if the pain gets worse or you vomit, consult your doctor.

SEE ALSO Diarrhoea and vomiting

Malnutrition

Even though a great deal of publicity is given to protein and vitamin deficiency, this is, in fact, a rare condition. Surplus nourishment, leading to obesity, is a more common nutritional problem. Another that is on the increase is food poisoning, mostly due to poor hygiene.

When undernourishment does occur, it is usually due to the complications of a disease such as depression or dementia. It also happens to someone who has difficulty in swallowing or has had a stomach operation. There are, in addition, social factors that contribute to malnutrition, such as a lack of money or when an older person is unable to prepare adequate meals because of living alone in an isolated area away from shops.

What you can do If you or someone you know, are at risk from malnutrition and have difficulty cooking, get in touch with the occupational therapist who may suggest kitchen modifications to make it easier to prepare meals. Some home helps do food shopping and cooking, and social services may be able to arrange for you to have meals on wheels. You could also ask for nutritional advice from a health visitor or a district nurse.

A daily diet should include the following: half a pint of skimmed milk or semi-skimmed if preferred; a piece of fruit for vitamin C; two slices of wholemeal bread or a portion of breakfast cereal rich in natural fibre; a portion of fish, meat, poultry, cheese or eggs (meat should only be eaten once a day). Oily fish (eg, sardines) is a good source of vitamin D and may protect against heart disease.

SEE ALSO Weight control

Medicines (use of)

As you get older, you may be taking a prescribed medicine to maintain your health (to regulate high blood pressure, for example) or to treat a short-term ailment. Medicines often contain powerful drugs, and may have serious unwanted effects if not used properly. Most medicines

come in child-resistant containers, so if you have difficulty in opening those, ask the pharmacist to supply an ordinary container instead.

What you can do   To use medicines safely, they should be taken exactly as prescribed. If they have been bought independently, the instructions on the label should be followed. Don't take medicines which have gone past the expiry date on the label.

Medicines you chose yourself or take on the advice of the pharmacist are not meant to be taken indefinitely. If they have not worked after five days, explain this to the pharmacist or consult your doctor.

As home remedies, keep the following items handy but out of reach of children: paracetamol, an antacid such as magnesium trisilicate and an antiseptic such as hydrogen peroxide.

Be careful about buying 'health remedies', herbal remedies and homoeopathic medicines, as these are also drugs; they may not agree with each other or with prescribed medicines. Check with your pharmacist or doctor, especially if you are taking prescribed medicines.

Dispose of medicines no longer needed. Flush them down the toilet or ask your pharmacist's advice.

Getting professional help   If instructions about taking medicines are not clear, ask the advice of a pharmacist. If you don't feel that a prescribed medicine is doing any good, do not stop taking it without asking the doctor's advice. The drug may be working even though you don't feel any immediate benefit.

If you notice a worrying side-effect, check with the pharmacist whether it is due to the medicine you are taking and whether you should continue taking it. If you receive repeat prescriptions, you should see your doctor in person every three months, unless a different timetable has been agreed.

Cost of medicines   NHS prescriptions are free for everyone over pension age. If you have diabetes, you can also get insulin syringes and needles free. The cost of private prescriptions depends on how expensive the medicine is.

Mental health

Research shows that the brain becomes unfit if it is not used, and like other areas of the body it needs regular stimulation. Retirement can lead to mental unfitness if nothing replaces the activity provided by work or the company of younger people, such as children and grandchildren. This mental activity is vital in preventing depression and anxiety.

What you can do   Various 'challenges' help maintain mental fitness, and these can be defined broadly as creative, intellectual, and personal.

Creativity is involved in a variety of everyday activities such as cooking, sewing and gardening. Creative challenge can extend to almost any area of living when you analyse what you are doing and learn something from it to apply elsewhere.

An intellectual challenge involves logic and memory when you do crosswords; play cards and Scrabble; read; learn a language or take an educational course. A personal challenge is involved when you take an active role in discussion groups or argue your case, perhaps at a local council or tenants' association meeting.

Mental illness   People who suffer from mental illness have the same thoughts and emotions that we all have, but theirs may be exaggerated and heightened. For example, we all get depressed at times; but when depression gets so severe that we cry, feel overwhelming anxiety, stop eating and sleeping, it becomes an illness. We have all been suspicious of things or people, but when such suspicions dominate thoughts and actions, we are mentally ill.

Although some mental diseases such as Alzheimer's can damage brain tissue, emotional health can be maintained: someone with dementia, for example, can be happy and interested in life. Stimulation is still needed, even though the person may be mentally ill. Highly skilled treatment from a psychiatrist, psychologist or social worker may be necessary, but the ill person also needs the help and encouragement of friends. Like everyone else, they need love and affection, company and discussion, respect and attention.

SEE ALSO Anxiety, Confusion, Depression

Osteoporosis

Women, more than men, are at risk of developing osteoporosis, the condition in which bones become more porous and brittle and more likely to break as a result of a fall. Osteoporosis may affect as many as a third of older women, especially if they: have white skin; are thin; have had premature menopause or have had both ovaries removed; are taking medicines such as corticosteroids or smoke. However, even if they belong to one of these categories, it does not automatically mean that osteoporosis will develop.

What you can do   There is a difference of medical opinion about whether taking extra calcium after the age of 70 slows down the rate at which your bones become more porous and brittle. The benefit of taking extra calcium is weak compared to that from hormone replacement therapy (HRT) taken at the time of the menopause. However, you may get enough calcium by drinking half a pint of milk a day (skimmed or semi-skimmed is fine, or one of the enriched calcium types of milk now available) and eating half a pound of low-fat cheese a week. You may also wish to ask the doctor about taking calcium tablets.

Getting professional help   Ask your doctor about hormone replacement therapy. If after discussion HRT is thought suitable, you will be prescribed medicines containing hormones to replace those that the body produces naturally before the menopause.

However, HRT helps prevent osteoporosis only when taken from the beginning of the menopause. If you have already developed osteoporosis, your doctor may be able to prescribe medicines that help build up bones, although, as with all medication, not everyone is a suitable subject for treatment.

Parkinson's Disease

It is not known exactly what causes Parkinson's Disease, which is characterised by a tremor or shaking, particularly noticeable in the hands when they are relaxed. Stiffness of movement, making the face appear expressionless, is another symptom as are slow movements. Because of these distressing symptoms, depression often accompanies Parkinson's Disease. Although the condition cannot yet be cured, sufferers can still lessen some of its effects and become both mentally and physically fitter.

What you can do   An important point is to continue to take any medication that has been prescribed. Missing doses will only make the symptoms worse. Constipation, which can sometimes be a problem, can be tackled in the natural way by eating fibrous foods. Laxatives are best avoided unless your doctor has advised them.

Because the tremor and movement difficulties associated with Parkinson's Disease may cause problems with dressing and eating, you may be helped by physiotherapy and by getting various aids to help with daily activities.

Getting professional help   Medical treatment is still aimed mainly at alleviating the symptoms and your doctor is the person to consult over that. Correctly prescribed medicine can help you maintain independence and be as comfortable as possible.

Sexuality

Even today, some people wrongly feel that it is not right for older people to enjoy making love with their partner, that somehow it is 'dirty'. Some older people themselves feel guilty about still wanting to make love, while others feel anxious that they no longer desire

intercourse. Anxiety or guilt feelings will affect someone's interest in sex. They can also make people feel depressed, adding still further to a loss of interest.

Sexual relations at any age are affected by many factors, both physical and psychological. Conditions such as arthritis or heart problems may make it difficult for someone to have intercourse as often as they would like. Medicines can also affect a person's ability or desire.

After the menopause, intercourse may be painful as the body produces less lubricating fluids in the vagina. Because they can no longer have children, some women may feel that lovemaking no longer has any point, even though the menopause bestows a new freedom on others, as they have no fear of becoming pregnant.

What you can do   At any age, what matters is how the two people involved feel about intercourse. There is no such thing as 'normal' frequency, whether you are young or old. A problem such as dryness can be dealt with by applying some lubricating gel, such as KY Jelly. Tender touching, without full intercourse, may be right for you in addition to talking with your partner about your sexual feelings. If you aren't used to discussing sex, you may be helped by talking about your inhibitions with someone you can relate to easily.

For more complete discussion of sexuality in later years, see *Living, Loving and Ageing* also published by Age Concern England and available from the address on page 78.

Getting professional help   You can get help with both physical and psychological problems connected with sex, provided you can overcome embarrassment and discuss the subject with your doctor. You may be referred to a local counselling service such as Relate whose national address is on page 70.

If medication has been contributing to sexual difficulties, you may be able to have it changed for another type without those side-effects. If you are disabled or wear a catheter because of incontinence and wonder how this will affect your sex life, contact SPOD at the address on page 71.

Skin

Skin changes are often the most noticeable signs of ageing particularly on the backs of hands, the face and the neck which are the areas of the body most exposed to the drying effects of wind, heat and sunlight. The brown 'liver' spots associated with ageing are harmless and come from an increase in pigmentation as a result of exposure to sun and wind.

What you can do   Excessive sunlight, cold winds, frequent contact with soap, water and household chemicals can all harm the skin. Wear rubber gloves to protect your hands from washing-up liquids, and also when doing gardening or car maintenance.

Even though exposure to sunshine helps your supply of vitamin D, do not allow your skin to be burned and use a good sunscreen, with a high protection factor, when you are in strong sunlight.

Dry skin also benefits from a moisturiser, preferably one that doesn't contain perfume. There is no medical evidence that so-called 'anti-ageing' creams affect skin cells: many such claims are not allowed in other countries and the most can be said of those preparations is that they are good moisturisers.

Getting professional help   For skin diseases such as dermatitis, eczema and ulcers, the earlier treatment is started, the more effective it is. See the doctor if: you develop an ulcer or other break in the skin; there is any marked changed in the size or appearance of a mole; there is itching, either localised or over the whole body; if you have red and weeping skin, including in the armpits, groin or under the breasts, and if any problem does not clear up within two weeks of home treatment.

SEE ALSO Cancer

Sleep

Many people say they seem to need less sleep as they grow older. This is not necessarily a problem, as long as you feel rested after sleeping, however short that is. If you are worried about losing sleep or find it difficult to get to sleep when you feel tired, it may help to develop a new sleeping pattern.

What you can do   There are a number of things you could try to help you fall asleep. Avoid naps during the day and go to bed about the same time every night, to help your body establish a regular sleeping time. Try to do some relaxing exercises before going to bed; or take the dog for a walk. Don't watch exciting television or read a stimulating book before retiring. Avoid tea or coffee, as these are stimulants, but have a nightcap of warm milk or a small glass of port or whisky at bedtime.

Getting professional help   If you are not sleeping because you are worried about something, try to talk it over with your doctor or someone you feel close to. If the doctor prescribes sleeping tablets, these should only be a short-term measure, as they can very quickly become addictive and you may become dependent upon them.

SEE ALSO Anxiety

Smoking

Smoking is a dangerous habit and causes many serious diseases, including lung cancer, bronchitis and artery problems. Giving up smoking improves health, no matter how long you have been smoking or whether you smoke cigarettes, cigars or a pipe.

What you can do   The best way to stop smoking is to give up completely, rather than trying to cut down gradually. Take up a new activity such as walking or swimming. Many people find it easier to stay off smoking if they have something that takes their mind off cigarettes. Analyse when you smoke – after a meal, perhaps – and try to break the habit by washing the dishes or going for a walk before you reach for a cigarette.

Getting professional help   Although stopping smoking depends greatly on will-power, there are a number of anti-smoking preparations on the market. The pharmacist, a doctor or a health visitor can advise you about these or where you may find an anti-smoking clinic in your area. Hypnosis and acupuncture have also helped some people, although such treatment is generally only available privately and may be expensive.

Stroke

The risk of suffering a stroke is increased by hardening of the arteries and by high blood pressure. When a stroke occurs, the blood supply to a part of the brain is cut off and the affected brain cells may die. The precise pattern of disability which occurs depends on the part of the brain affected.

A stroke often affects sufferers' ability to think logically, and there may be speech difficulties as well. It is not fully known why some strokes occur, but the risk of having one can sometimes be prevented. If you have already had a stroke, that does not mean you are likely to have another; only a minority of people suffer a second stroke.

What you can do Have your blood pressure checked regularly. Naturally, if you are receiving treatment for high blood pressure, continue to take the medication prescribed.

There are ways in which the chances of having a second stroke can be reduced. You should ask your doctor about taking aspirin, which in this condition acts not as a pain killer but as a drug that reduces the risk of a blood clot. You can also help yourself by remaining as active as possible and trying to maintain an optimistic outlook on life.

Getting professional help After a stroke, your doctor may be able to arrange for physiotherapy or for you to attend a day hospital to help prevent unnecessary disability. To improve speech and communication, you should contact the speech therapy services direct, through the health authority's district speech therapist. There are also local stroke clubs where volunteers help with speech and other problems. Contact can be made with one of these through the Chest, Heart and Stroke Association at the address on page 64.

Weight control

Life doesn't seem fair to some people: they watch what they eat, deny themselves things like chips, cakes and chocolate and still put on weight, whereas other people eat what they want and never put on a pound. Whether or not you put on weight easily, the cause of obesity is that you consume more energy than you are using, and the surplus is being converted into fat.

A few of the ways in which being overweight can affect your health in middle and old age are the risk of developing high blood pressure, heart disease and diabetes; the burden of extra weight if you have arthritis; the risk of falling because of decreased mobility.

What you can do   To lose weight slowly – for example, to take off seven pounds over a period of a year or to keep your weight steady – you need to change the balance of your diet and eat fewer calories. Sugar and fat are the most energy-rich foods and provide calories in a concentrated form.

Avoiding fats   Choose the healthier polyunsaturated fats we hear about so frequently these days, which are a form of unsaturated fat. Apart from leading to overweight, too much saturated fat in your diet raises the cholesterol level in the arteries which contributes to heart disease.

The main sources of saturated fats are: full-fat milk, most hard and full-fat cream cheeses; butter, lard, dripping, suet; meat products (pies, salami, pâté, sausages); cakes, biscuits, fried foods, chips.

Some good alternatives are: semi-skimmed or skimmed milk; natural yoghurt, reduced-fat cream and hard cheeses, Edam, cottage cheese, curd cheese, low-fat soft cheeses; fish (fresh or tinned, drained of oil); lean mince, reduced-fat sausages and pâtés, offal, chicken and turkey (skin removed); breads and scones made with polyunsaturated fat; polyunsaturated margarine or low-fat spread; corn or soya oils.

Watch out for sugar   Eating too many sweet foods contributes to being overweight. Sugar also encourages tooth decay and gum disease

and provides empty calories – that is, fattening ones without other valuable nutrients. You don't need sugar for energy, as all food provides it; and you will get all you need from fresh fruit.

The main sources of sugar are: packet sugar used in cooking and at the table; cakes, biscuits, sweets, chocolates; soft and alcoholic drinks; canned fruit in syrup, fruit yoghurts.

Some good alternatives are: artificial sweeteners; homemade breads and scones made with little or no sugar; fresh or dried fruit; unsalted nuts; low-calorie, 'dry' alcoholic drinks, mineral water; fruit canned in natural juice, plain yoghurts.

By choosing from these alternative sources of fat and sugar, you will not go hungry and will be eating a balanced diet with enough fibre and vitamins.

Getting professional help To lose weight quickly – for example, seven or eight pounds in three weeks – you need a special low-calorie diet. There are many slimming books available, but if your attempts with a book do not work, you could ask your doctor who may advise a special diet or recommend a dietetic clinic at the local health centre.

SEE ALSO Constipation, Malnutrition

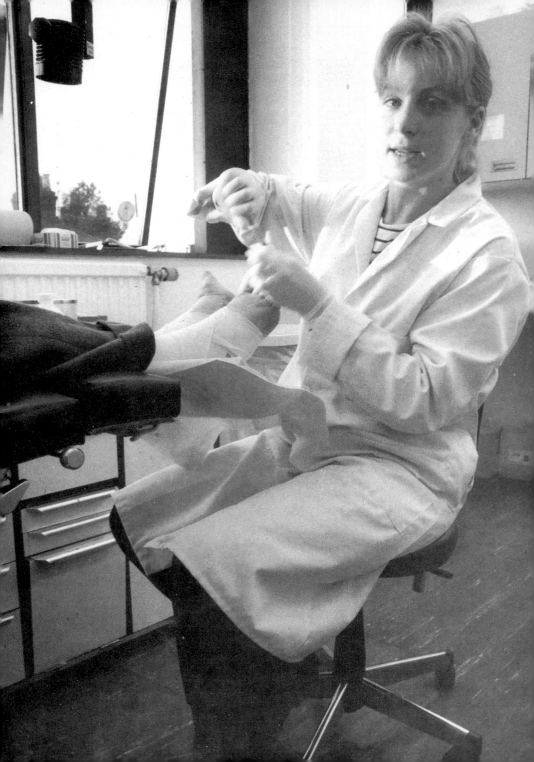

F U R T H E R

INFORMATION

The people listed in this section of the book are grouped according to whether they work for the National Health Service, the local authority or whether they provide complementary medical treatment. There are also voluntary health and social services provided by local agencies.

The organisations listed on pages 61 to 72 are mostly national, but many have local branches or can put you in touch with local groups where you can get help and support. All the organisations referred to in 'An A to Z' are included, but there are also many others. You could ask about them at your local library or Age Concern group.

The Reading List on page 73 contains details about books and leaflets.

People to Help You

Health Services

There is a wide variety of individuals and services to help with your health problems. However, not every area in the country will offer all the National Health Services described in this section, and there may be a long waiting list for an appointment or for some form of care.

If you find it difficult to get a service you need through the NHS, get in touch with the Community Health Council (CHC), which represents the interests of the consumer and will provide help and guidance. The CHC will also help you to make a formal complaint and guide you through any official procedures. Don't be afraid to demand an adequate service. The CHC will be listed in the telephone directory under the district health authority.

If you have a complaint about the service provided by a doctor, get in touch with the Family Practitioner Committee (FPC) in your area. To change your doctor or dentist, ask them for a list of local practitioners. The FPC will be listed separately as the Family Practitioner Committee in the telephone directory. The FPC also oversees dentists, opticians and pharmacists in each area.

Care attendants

They are trained to substitute for carers who are looking after someone at home. They may help with housework and provide nursing care. Get in touch with the district health authority or the social services department to find out whether there is a care attendant scheme in your area. You can also contact the Crossroads Care Attendant Schemes at the address on page 64.

Chiropodists

They work usually in their own consulting rooms, in clinics held in health centres, or in old people's homes. They also make home visits, although treatment is preferable in a clinic where they have all their equipment to hand.

The NHS chiropody service can be contacted directly by looking in the telephone directory under chiropody or the name of the district health authority. As the service is in very short supply and in some areas the waiting list is very long, many people choose private treatment. In any case, you should make sure that the chiropodist is state registered and has the letters SRCh after his or her name, as there are no regulations governing non-registered practitioners.

Community psychiatric nurses

They are trained to deal with mental health problems and visit people at home to provide advice and practical help. The availability of psychiatric nurses varies widely – in some areas they are in very short supply, while in others they provide a 24-hour service. They are contactable through the GP, the hospital psychiatrist or a geriatrician.

Continence advisers

They are specially trained nurses who can help manage incontinence, whether bowel or urinary, and tell you about useful aids and how to get them.

Not every health authority has a continence adviser, but your doctor or health visitor will know about this. Otherwise get in touch with the Association of Continence Advisers at the Disabled Living Foundation (address on page 65).

Dentists

They work mainly from their surgeries, but you may be able to get a home visit from the community dental service if you are housebound. This service can be contacted through your doctor or health visitor.

If you have problems in finding an NHS dentist, get advice from the local family practitioner committee or the community health council.

For information about dental charges, see page 19.

District nurses

They have taken extra training after qualification and provide home care such as treating leg ulcers, giving injections and terminal care. They can also advise about incontinence and arrange for useful aids. They usually work with nursing auxiliaries as part of the primary health care team and can be contacted at the GP's surgery, local health centre or the district health authority.

Many district nurses also advise on home nursing aids and teach carers how to lift someone.

General practitioners

They provide treatment, information, support and referral to other medical and nursing services. Most GPs will make home visits if necessary.

If you need to register with a GP or are not satisfied with the service offered, ask locally whether there is a GP who might meet your requirements – for instance, for a surgery with access for a wheelchair. The family practitioner committee will also have a list of local doctors.

Health visitors

They are nurses who have taken extra training in preventive medicine. They can advise about practical ways of coping with difficulties and local services available to help people with social, financial or housing problems. They do not undertake nursing tasks.

Some health visitors work particularly with elderly people through the GP's surgery. They can also be approached directly at the local health centre or through the district health authority.

Hearing aid technicians

They are trained in the assessment and supplying of hearing aids and in helping people adjust to using them. Contact the technician through the hospital ear, nose and throat (ENT) or audiology clinic.

Hospital staff

They comprise another important group of people who work for the NHS. Junior hospital doctors, housemen or registrars, who are on the wards most of the time, should be able to answer questions about a particular disease or the treatment. If you are a relative of a patient and wish to discuss a problem, ask to speak to one of these doctors.

There are also senior doctors with specialist training – like orthopaedic surgeons, psychiatrists, psychogeriatricians – who are usually consultants and supervise treatment. Geriatricians are consultants who work with other hospital staff to offer a special service for older people.

Dieticians can be contacted at a hospital out-patient clinic for a condition such as obesity and diabetes or if you are recovering from an operation or illness and need a special diet.

Ward sisters or staff nurses can give advice about an illness and explain the doctor's information if that is not clear. They can also advise on practical problems and worries about hospital after-care.

Opticians

They work mainly in their high street premises, though some make home visits for an extra charge. Opthalmic opticians also carry out sight tests, for which they can now charge. The community health council or local family practitioner committee will have information about opticians prepared to make home visits. For information about vouchers towards the cost of glasses and charges for eye tests, see page 30.

Pharmacists

They can give advice on medicines, whether prescribed or bought over the counter. They should be consulted especially if you intend to buy a particular medicine and are also taking something prescribed by the GP or a hospital doctor. Ask to speak to the pharmacist personally, as a shop assistant is unlikely to be qualified to give advice.

Physiotherapists

They treat disorders of the muscles and joints with massage, heat and exercise. They also give advice and information about aids such as a walking frame or a wheelchair. Most 'physios' work in hospitals, but in some areas there is a community service for home visits. If there is none where you live, contact the physiotherapy department at the local hospital.

Speech therapists

They are trained to diagnose and treat language disorders such as speech difficulties that may result from a stroke. They work mainly in hospitals, schools and clinics and can be contacted through the district health authority.

Although it is not necessary to be referred by a GP or health visitor, they can help get an appointment with a speech therapist, as this service is in very short supply in many parts of the country.

Voluntary services

Local groups such as the Red Cross, the Women's Royal Voluntary Service (WRVS) and Age Concern may offer day care for frail older people and assistance for someone who has just been discharged from hospital. In addition these organisations may have wheelchairs for an emergency loan and offer help with home nursing and bathing.

Age Concern England also has information about local health promotion activity as part of its Age Well Programme. Write to Age Well c/o Age Concern England at the address on page 78.

Complementary Medical Practitioners

Once you have investigated a medical problem through the NHS and have been told that the treatment suggested is all that can be done, you may want to try complementary medicine. In addition to the therapies described in this section, there are Herbalists and practitioners of the Alexander Technique.

Though complementary medicine is becoming increasingly popular, you should note whether the practitioner you choose is registered with an official organisation, as there are people who charge unreasonably high fees.

Acupuncturists

They use very fine needles at special points on the meridian system to affect a stimulating or sedating effect on the vital energy of the body. A balance of energy is vital to human health. The special points are mainly on the surface of the skin. Massage is also used in acupuncture in addition to moxa, a herbal preparation used to heat the needles for a helpful reaction. For thousands of years acupuncture has been an approved treatment in Chinese medical circles.

Because there is no system of compulsory registration for Acupuncturists in the UK, anyone can claim to be one. However, the members of the British Acupuncture Association are qualified and can be contacted through the association at the address on page 62. The Traditional Acupuncture Society requires formal training and ensures the professional and ethical standards of its members. Write to the society at the address on page 71.

Chiropractors

The main condition which chiropractors treat is backache, but they can help in the treatment of joint disorders as well. Chiropractors manipulate joints by hand to rebalance the body.

If the GP, or an orthopaedic surgeon, says that he or she can do no more for your backache, ask to be referred to an osteopath or chiropractor. If the referral is refused, ask whether there is a medical reason for this.

In reverse, a properly trained chiropractor or osteopath should recognise conditions which are better treated by conventional medicine and will refer you to a suitable practitioner. The letters DC after the chiropractor's name stand for Doctor of Chiropractic. However, anyone can use those letters, whether or not they have had training, so it is wise to choose a member of the British Chiropractic Association, as it admits only fully trained chiropractors. Write to the association at the address on page 62.

SEE ALSO Osteopaths

Homoeopaths

They are qualified doctors who have special training in homoeopathy. They prescribe natural mineral, plant and animal substances in minute quantities which stimulate the body's ability to heal.

If you are worried about the drugs used in manufactured medicines, homoeopathy with its emphasis on the natural source of remedies may be more attractive to you. However, if a disorder would be better treated by surgery or manufactured drugs, most homoeopathic doctors will refer you to a surgeon or use conventional drug therapy.

Homoeopathic medicine is available on the NHS, but there are very few specially trained doctors practising within the NHS. To choose one near you or to get the address of a homoeopathic pharmacy, write to the British Homoeopathic Association, at the address on page 63. You can also ask to be referred to an NHS Homoeopathic Hospital.

Naturopaths

They treat many disorders including stomach trouble, asthma and hay fever with natural therapy such as regular exercise and a healthy diet. Naturopathy may be combined with osteopathy, but the two types of treatment are usually given independently for different types of complaints. Recommended naturopaths are those with the letters ND MRN (Diploma of Naturopathy and Member of the General Council and Register of Naturopaths). For the address of a registered naturopath, write to the General Council at the address on page 65.

SEE ALSO Osteopaths

Osteopaths

They practice in much the same way as chiropractors but treat the whole body. Registered osteopaths have the following letters after their names: DO and MRO (Diploma in Osteopathy and Member of the Register of Osteopaths). For the name of a registered osteopath in your area, write to the General Council and Register of Osteopaths at the address on page 66.

SEE ALSO Chiropractors and Naturopaths

Social Services

The availability of social services varies greatly around the country. You can find the telephone number of your local Social Services Department (called Social Work Department in Scotland) by looking in the telephone directory under the name of your local authority (county or London borough).

If you want to complain about a local social service, contact the Director of the Social Services Department or a local councillor.

Home helps

They do light housework, collect pensions, shop or prepare meals for someone who is ill or has just been discharged from hospital. How much assistance they give depends on the person's circumstances and whether they are also supported by friends and relatives. Many local authorities make a charge for the service.

In some areas of the country home helps will give more personal care like help with getting up and dressing and are called homecare workers or domiciliary carers.

SEE ALSO Care attendants

Occupational therapists

They work both in hospitals and in the community and have been trained to teach people with disabilities and those who care for them how to manage daily tasks. They can also advise about aids and adaptations to the home and how to get them. For people on low incomes who need help with paying for adaptations, the OT will advise about any grant aid and the procedures involved in getting it.

OTs are also called advisers to the handicapped or rehabilitation officers.

Social workers

They are trained to help with emotional and social problems and are usually based in area teams. Some work in hospitals or are attached to health centres and act as a link between the health and social services. A social worker may be able to arrange for other services such as a home help, day care, meals on wheels or residential accommodation.

Some specialist social workers give advice on aids and equipment for those who are deaf, hard of hearing or partially sighted.

Voluntary services

In many areas of the country, voluntary organisations work with local authorities to run luncheon clubs, meals on wheels as well as day centres and recreational activities for retired people. Contact the local Age Concern group, WRVS or Citizens Advice Bureau.

Useful Organisations

*The London dialling code changes in April 1990 to either 071 – or 081 –
depending on the area. Please check all London numbers listed here with your
operator.*

A

Age Concern England
See full description on page 78.

Bernard Sunley House
60 Pitcairn Road
Mitcham, Surrey CR4 3LL
Tel: 081-640 5431

Age Concern Northern Ireland

6 Lower Crescent
Belfast BT7 1NR
Tel: 0232 245729

Age Concern Scotland

54a Fountainbridge
Edinburgh EH3 9PT
Tel: 031-228 5656

Age Concern Wales

4th Floor
1 Cathedral Road
Cardiff CF1 9SD
Tel: 0222 371821/371566

Alzheimer's Disease Society
*For local groups and a guide for
caring for someone with
dementia.*

158-160 Balham High Road
London SW12 9BN
Tel: 01-675 6557

Alcohol Concern
*Information and details of local
services and groups.*

305 Gray's Inn Road
London WC1X 8QF
Tel: 01-833 3471

Arthritis Care
*Information and advice on
benefits and holidays.*

5 Grosvenor Crescent
London SW1X 7ER
Tel: 01-235 0902

**Association of Teachers of Lipreading
to Adults**
For list of teachers.

Jenny Harris
c/o The Post Office
Slimbridge
Gloucester

B

**Breastcare and Mastectomy
Association of GB**
*Information and services on
non-medical matters.*

26 Harrison Street
off Gray's Inn Road
London WC1H 8JG
Tel: 01-837 0908

BACUP (British Association of
Cancer United Patients)
*Information service and details of
developments in treatment.*

121-123 Charterhouse Street
London EC1M 6AA
Tel: 01-608 1661
or   0800 1811991

**British Acupuncture Association
and Register**
*Provides list of members on
receipt of SAE and £1.50.*

34 Alderney Street
London SW1V 4EU
Tel: 01-834 1012/3353

**British Association of the Hard of
Hearing**
*Information and advice, local
clubs.*

7-11 Armstrong Road
London W3 7JL
Tel: 01-743 1110/1353

British Chiropractic Association
*Will send list of practitioners on
receipt of SAE and £1.00.
Produces publications.*

Premier House
10 Greycoat Place
London SW1T 1SB
Tel: 01-222 8866

British Deaf Association
Information, local activities.
Also runs courses and holidays.

38 Victoria Place
Carlisle
Cumbria CA1 1HU
Tel: 0228 48844

British Diabetic Association
Information and literature; local
branches and self-help groups.

10 Queen Anne Street
London W1M 0BD
Tel: 01-323 1531

British Homoeopathic Association
List of medically qualified
practitioners, pharmacies,
manufacturers. Runs self-help
courses.

27a Devonshire Street
London W1N 1RJ
Tel: 01-935 2163

British Sports Association for the
Disabled
Information on classes and
centres.

Mary Clen Haig Suite
34 Osnaburgh Street
London NW1 3ND
Tel: 01-383 7277

British T'ai Chi Chuan Association
Information and instruction.

7 Upper Wimpole Street
London W1M 7TD
Tel: 01-935 8444

Brittle Bone Society
Advice and information service
and some financial help.

Unit 4, Block 20
Carlunie Road
Dunsimane Estate
Dundee DD2 3QT
Tel: 0382 67603

Cancer Link
Information and support through
local groups.

17 Britannia Street
London WC1X 9JN
Tel: 01-833 2451

Carers' National Association
Support, information and local
groups.

29 Chilworth Mews
London W2 3RG
Tel: 01-724 7776

Chest, Heart and Stroke Association
Literature and advice, network of clubs.

Tavistock House North
Tavistock Square
London WC1H 9JE
Tel: 01-387 3012

College of Health
Literature and information. Promotes self-care through self-help groups.

18 Victoria Park Square
Bethnal Green
London E2 9PF
Tel: 01-980 6263

Crossroads (Association of Crossroads Care Attendant Schemes)
Provides trained home care for ill or disabled people. Network of local schemes.

10 Regent Place
Rugby
Warwickshire CV21 2PN
Tel: 0788 73653

CRUSE – Bereavement Care
Information, counselling and local support groups.

126 Sheen Road
Richmond
Surrey TW9 1UR
Tel: 01-940 4818/9047

Depressives Association
Information and local support.

PO Box 5
Castletown
Portland
Dorset DT5 1BQ

Dial UK (Disablement Information Advice Line)
Information packs for disabled people. Local branches throughout UK.

117 High Street
Clay Cross
Chesterfield
Derbyshire S45 9DZ
Tel: 0246 250 055

Disability Alliance
Campaigns for disabled people, publishes Disability Rights Handbook.

25 Denmark Street
London WC2H 8NJ
Tel: 01-240 0806

Disabled Living Foundation
*Comprehensive information
service, Continence Advisory
Service.*

380-384 Harrow Road
London W9 2HU
Tel: 01-289 6111

Extend (Exercise Training for the
Elderly or Disabled)
*Local groups, instructions,
exercise booklets and cassettes.*

1A North Street
Sheringham
Norfolk NR26 8LJ
Tel: 0263 822479

Eyecare Information Bureau
Leaflets and advice.

Bridge House
232-234 Blackfriars Road
London SE1 8NW
Tel: 01-928 9435

FREE (Forum for the Rights of Elderly
People to Education)
*Provides information on all
aspects of education for older
people.*

c/o Age Concern England
60 Pitcairn Road
Mitcham, Surrey CR4 3LL
Tel: 081-640 5431

Gay Bereavement Project
Information and support.

Unitarian Rooms
Hoop Lane
London NW11 8BS
Tel: 01-455 8894

**General Council and Register of
Naturopaths**
*List of members on receipt of SAE
and £1.50.*

6 Netherhall Gardens
London NW3 5RR
Tel: 01-435 8728

General Council and Register of Osteopaths
List of registered osteopaths.

56 London Street
Reading, Berks RG1 4SQ
Tel: 0734 576585

Health Education Authority
Publishes booklets and information.

Hamilton House
Mabledon Place
London WC1H 9TX
Tel: 01-631 0930

Healthline
Runs 24-hour free health information service. Also provides list of subjects covered on tape.

PO Box 499
London E2 9PU
Tel: 01-980 4848
(to listen to tapes)

Hearing Aid Council
Advice and information on aids.

Moorgate House
201 Silbury Field Boulevard
Milton Keynes MK9 1LZ
Tel: 0908 585442

Help the Aged
Literature and information.

16-18 St James's Walk
London EC1R 0BE
Tel: 01-253 0253

Holiday Care Service
Information on holidays for disabled and older people. Also runs Holiday Helpers Scheme.

2 Old Bank Chambers
Station Road
Horley
Surrey RH6 9HW
Tel: 0293 774535

Institute of Complementary Medicine
Charity and information centre. Send SAE for local practitioners.

21 Portland Place
London W1N 3AF
Tel: 01-636 9543

International Glaucoma Association
Provides leaflets and information.

Ophthalmology Department
Kings College Hospital
Denmark Hill
London SE5 9RS
Tel: 01-274 6222 ext 2934

Jewish Bereavement Counselling Service
Trained volunteers offer visiting service.

Woburn House
4 Upper Woburn Place
London WC1H OEZ
Tel: 01-349 0839 *24-hour service*
01-387 4300 ext 227 *office hours*

Jewish Marriage Council
For advice and help on marital problems.

23 Ravenshurst Avenue
London NW4 4EL
Tel: 01-203 6311

Keep Fit Association
For addresses of local classes and leaflets on exercises.

16 Upper Woburn Place
London WC1H 0QG
Tel: 01-387 4349

London College of Osteopathic Medicine
For medically qualified practitioners and details of clinics.

8-10 Boston Place
London NW1 6QH
Tel: 01-262 5250/1128

MIND (National Association for Mental Health)
Literature, information, advice on legal and welfare rights. Also has local groups.

22 Harley Street
London W1N 2ED
Tel: 01-637 0741

Bookshop
24-32 Stephenson Way
London NW1 2HD

National Association for Widows
Information and support.

54-57 Allison Street
Digbeth
Birmingham B5 5TH
Tel: 021-643 8348

National Back Pain Association
For details of local groups, send SAE.

31-33 Park Road
Teddington
Middlesex TW11 OAB
Tel: 01-977 5474

National Institute of Medical Herbalists
For list of practising doctors and herbal suppliers.

Miss Janet Hicks
41 Hatherley Road
Winchester
Hampshire SO22 6RR
Tel: 0962 68776

National Osteoporosis Society
Information and advice.

PO Box 10
Barton Meade House
Radstock
Bath BA3 3YB
Tel: 0761 32472

National Society for Cancer Relief
For information and practical help.

Anchor House
15-19 Britten Street
London SW3 3TZ
Tel: 01-351 7811

Northern Ireland Association for Mental Health
See entry for MIND.

84 University Street
Belfast BT7 1HE
Tel: 0232 328474

Northern Ireland Council on Disability
Information and advice.

2 Annadale Avenue
Belfast BY7 3JR
Tel: 0232 4919011

Optical Information Council
Information and leaflets.

19-24 Temple Chambers
Temple Avenue
London EC4Y 0DT
Tel: 01-353 3556

Parkinson's Disease Society of the UK
Self-help groups, information and advice.

36 Portland Place
London W1N 3DG
Tel: 01-323 1174

Partially Sighted Society
Network of local groups and large print publications.

206 Gt Portland Street
London W1N 6AA
Tel: 01-387 8840
or
Queens Road
Doncaster
South Yorkshire DN1 2NX
Tel: 0302 368998

RADAR (Royal Association for Disability and Rehabilitation)
Information and help on welfare services, access and holidays.

25 Mortimer Street
London W1N 8AB
Tel: 01-637 5400

Relaxation for Living
Large SAE for information, literature, tapes, details about classes.

29 Burwood Park Road
Walton-on-Thames
Surrey KT12 5LH

Relate (formerly National Marriage Guidance Council)
Publishes books and runs counselling service. Local branches.

Herbert Grey College
Little Church Street
Rugby CV21 3AP
Tel: 0788 73241

RoSPA (Royal Society for the Prevention of Accidents)
Information, publishes Safety in Retirement.

Cannon House
The Priory
Queensway
Birmingham B4 6BS
Tel: 021-200 2461

Royal National Institute for the Blind
Wide range of information, services, equipment for blind and partially sighted people. Also runs Talking Book Service.

224 Great Portland Street
London W1N 6AA
Tel: 01-388 1266

Royal National Institute for the Deaf
Wide range of services and advice.

105 Gower Street
London WC1E 6AH
Tel: 01-387 8033

S

Scottish Association for Mental Health
See entry for MIND.

Atlantic House
38 Gardner's Crescent
Edinburgh EH3 8DG
Tel: 031-229 9687

Society of Chiropodists
List of State Registered Chiropodists. Information about foot care.

53 Welbeck Street
London W1M 7HE
Tel: 01-486 3381
(2-4 pm Tues & Thurs)

Scottish Council on Disability
  Information department offers
  24-hour service.

Princes House
5 Shandwick Place
Edinburgh EH2 4RG
Tel: 031-229 8632

SPOD (Association to Aid the Sexual
and Personal Relationships of People
with Disabilities)
  For information and contact with
  relevant counsellors.

286 Camden Road
London N7 0BJ
Tel: 01-607 8851

Sports Council
  For information about 50-plus
  sports campaign.

16 Upper Woburn Place
London WC1H OQP
Tel: 01-388 1277

Traditional Acupuncture Society
  Details of practitioners.

1 The Ridgeway
Stratford upon Avon
Warwickshire CV37 9SL
Tel: 0789 298798

Tranx UK Ltd (National Tranquilliser
Advisory Council)
  Advice and support for users of
  tranquillisers. Self-help groups.

25A Masons Avenue
Wealdstone, Harrow
Middlesex HA3 5AH
Tel: 01-427 2065

University of the Third Age
  Large SAE for information on
  educational activities for retired
  people. Has local branches
  according to interest.

c/o BASSAC
13 Stockwell Road
London SW9 9AU
Tel: 01-737 2541

Wales Council for the Disabled
Information and advice.

Llys Ifor
Crescent Road
Caerphilly
Mid Glamorgan CF8 1XL
Tel: 0222 887325

Women's League of Health and Beauty
Details of local clubs/classes.

Walter House
418-422 Strand
London WC2R 0PT
Tel: 01-240 8456

Women's National Cancer Control Campaign
Information on cervical and breast screening. Mobile clinics.

1 South Audley Street
London W1Y 5DQ
Tel: 01-499 7532
    01-495 4995 *Helpline*

Reading List

Publications from Age Concern England are described on pages 74-77.

Free factsheets are available from Age Concern England's Information and Policy Department. Send a 9" × 5" sae to the address on page 78. Factsheets about health topics are *Dental Care in Retirement* and *Help with Incontinence*.

The Department of Social Security publishes a wide range of free leaflets, available from their local offices or from branches of the Citizens Advice Bureau and local post offices. You may want to ask for one of the following leaflets:

HB 1   *Services and Benefits for Disabled People*
HB 2   *Equipment for Disabled People*
HB 4   *Help with Mobility: Getting Around*

The King's Fund and the Health Education Authority have published a handbook called *Caring at Home*. For details about price and ordering contact the National Extension College, 18 Brooklands Avenue, Cambridge CB2 2HN, tel: 0223 316644.

The Optical Information Council (address on page 69) publishes free written information about eye care including *Eye Care and the Elderly* and *Eye Care after Cataracts*.

Age Concern Greater London publishes free information about counselling and services in the London area for people experiencing sexual problems. Send a 9" × 5" sae to them at 43 Knatchbull Road, London SE5 9QY, tel: 01-737 3456.

Publications from Age Concern England

A wide range of titles are available under the Age Concern imprint.

Health

The Magic of Movement Laura Mitchell **£3.95**

0-86242-076-8

Full of encouragement, this book by TV personality Laura Mitchell is for those who are finding everyday activities more difficult. Includes gentle exercises to tone up muscles and ideas to make you more independent and avoid boredom.

Know Your Medicines Pat Blair **£3.95**

0-86242-043-1

This guide for older people and their carers explains how the body works and how it is affected by medication. Also included is guidance on using medicines and an index of commonly used medicines and their side effects.

The Foot Care Book : An A-Z of fitter feet Judith Kemp SRCh **£2.95**

0-86242-066-0

A self-help guide for older people on routine foot care, this book includes an A-Z of problems, information on adapting and choosing shoes and a guide to who's who in foot care.

In Touch With Cataracts Margaret Ford **£1.00**

0-86242-037-7

Over 20,000 cataract operations take place each year. Some patients have difficulties in adapting to their new vision. This booklet looks at ways of solving some of the problems and aims to allay anxieties.

Management of Continence for older people and their carers will be published in the second half of 1990. Write to the Marketing Department at Age Concern England for details.

Housing

Housing Options For Older People David Bookbinder **£2.50**

0-86242-055-5

A review of housing options is part of growing older. All the possibilities and their practical implications are carefully considered in this comprehensive guide.

Sharing Your Home Christine Orton **£1.95**

0-86242-060-1

Guidelines for multi-generational families considering living together under the same roof. Includes information about the legal and financial factors as well as the emotional adjustments required.

A Buyer's Guide To Sheltered Housing Co-published with the NHTPC **£2.50**

0-86242-063-6

Buying a flat or bungalow in a sheltered scheme? This guide provides vital information on the running costs, location, design and management of schemes to help you make an informed decision.

At Home In A Home Pat Young **£3.95**

0-86242-062-8

The questions older people ask when considering moving into residential accommodation are answered in this practical guide. Such topics as fees, financial support and standards of care are tackled in realistic terms in order to help people make the right choice.

Money Matters

Your Rights Sally West   **£1.50***

0-86242-080-6

A highly acclaimed annual guide to the State benefits available to older people. Contains current information on retirement pensions, means-tested benefits as well as other financial help in paying for health and residential care, transport and legal fees.

Your Taxes and Savings John Burke and Sally West   **£2.70***

0-86242-081-4

Explains how the tax system affects people over retirement age, includes advice on independent taxation and how to avoid paying more tax than necessary. The information about savings covers the wide range of investment opportunities now available. The book is updated annually.

Using Your Home As Capital Cecil Hinton   **£2.50***

0-86242-084-9

This best selling book for home-owners, which is updated annually, gives a detailed explanation of how to capitalise on the value of your home and obtain a regular additional income.

General

Living, Loving and Ageing: Sexual and personal relationships in later life Wendy Greengross and Sally Greengross   **£4.95**

0-86242-070-9

Sexuality is often regarded as the preserve of the younger generation. At last, here is a book for older people, and those who care for them, which tackles the issues in a straightforward fashion, avoiding preconceptions and bias.

Famous Ways To Grow Old Philip Bristow   **£8.95**
0-86242-087-3

A collection of letters from a host of internationally distinguished figures, outlining their personal attitudes to the onset of old age. Full of amusing and touching anecdotal material. Contributors include: James Callaghan; Peggy Ashcroft; Cardinal Basil Hume and Barbara Cartland.

Survival Guide For Widows June Hemer and Ann Stanyer   **£3.50**
0-86242-049-0

Widows describe what grieving has meant to them. Other people with experience of the practical side of widowhood give guidance on Wills, taxation, social security, housing and living alone.

What Every Woman Should Know About Retirement Edited by Helen Franks   **£4.50**
0-86242-054-7

Retirement for women may appear less drastic a change than for men but it is, in many ways, more complex, affecting many parts of their lives. These include marriage, living alone, financial planning, caring for someone, looking after health and appearance.

Life In The Sun: A guide to long-stay holidays and living abroad in retirement Nancy Tuft   **£6.95**
0-86242-085-7

Every year millions of older people consider either taking long-stay holidays or moving abroad on a more permanent basis. This essential guide examines the pitfalls associated with such a move and tackles topics varying from pets to poll tax.

*Please check current price before purchase.

If you would like to order any of these titles, send a cheque or money order to Department YH1, Age Concern England, 60 Pitcairn Road, Mitcham, Surrey CR4 3LL.

About Age Concern

This is one of a wide range of publications produced by Age Concern England – the NATIONAL COUNCIL ON AGEING. In addition, Age Concern England is also actively engaged in training, information provision, research and campaigning for retired people and those who work with them. It is a registered charity dependent on public support for the continuation of its work.

Age Concern England links closely with Age Concern centres in Scotland, Wales and Northern Ireland to form a network of over 1400 independent local UK groups. These groups, with the invaluable help of an estimated 250,000 volunteers, aim to improve the quality of life for older people and develop services appropriate to local needs and resources. These include advice and information, day care, visiting services, transport schemes, clubs, and specialist facilities for physically and mentally frail older people.

In particular, through its Age Well programme, initiated jointly with the Health Education Authority, Age Concern England is actively involved in promoting a healthier old age.

Age Concern England
Bernard Sunley House
60 Pitcairn Road
Mitcham
Surrey CR4 3LL
Tel: 081-640 5431

Age Concern Scotland
54a Fountainbridge
Edinburgh EH3 9PT
Tel: 031-228 5656

Age Concern Wales
4th Floor
1 Cathedral Road
Cardiff CF1 9SD
Tel: 0222 371821/371566

Age Concern Northern Ireland
6 Lower Crescent
Belfast BT7 1NR
Tel: 0232 245729

We hope you found this book useful. If so, perhaps you would like to receive further information about Age Concern or help us do more for elderly people.

Dear Age Concern
Please send me the details I've ticked below:

other publications

☐

Age Concern special offers

☐

volunteer with a local group

☐

regular giving

☐

covenant

☐

legacy

☐

Meantime, here is a gift of

£ _____ PO/CHEQUE or VISA/ACCESS No _____

NAME (BLOCK CAPITALS) _____

SIGNATURE _____

ADDRESS _____

_____

_____ POSTCODE _____

Please pull out this page and send it to: **Age Concern** (DEPT. YH1)
FREEPOST
Mitcham,
no stamp needed **Surrey CR4 9AS**